Lizard loses his tail

Story by Beverley Randell
Illustrated by Bruce Lauchlan

Here is Lizard.

He is asleep in the sun.

Kingfisher is in the tree.

6

Kingfisher is hungry.

He is looking for a lizard.

Lizard wakes up.

Look!

Here comes Kingfisher.

Here comes Kingfisher.
Away goes Lizard.
Look at Lizard's tail!

Lizard is going home.

He is **safe**.

Where is Lizard's tail?

Kingfisher
is **eating**
Lizard's tail.